David Chorlton

SELECTED POEMS

FUTURECYCLE PRESS

www.futurecycle.org

Published by FutureCycle Press
Lexington, Kentucky, USA

ISBN 978-1-938853-58-6

The farther behind I leave the past, the closer I am to forging my own character.

—Isabelle Eberhardt

Contents

RECENT

Acknowledgments

A Retrospective

A conventional approach to a "Selected" book of poems features a generous selection from the author's books with, perhaps, some newer work to complete the volume. The more I looked at my own options, the less inclined I was to make choices of what I thought to be simply the best, which would always lead me back to certain titles I had often featured for some reason in my readings. The project was losing its gloss for me, until I decided to make my selections on the basis of my recollections that, in writing specific poems over more than thirty years, a moment of illumination eased the process along and invariably prepared the way for some of what was to come. As themes come and go, I hope the more recent work shows a few more flashes of intuition giving life to the writing.

—D. C.

SELECTIONS

Smoky Tango

This river has no mercy. Dry
with the dust of dreams, it is
an artery, leading not
to the heart but the drastic outskirts
of our city. A rose of steel

has grown here, a labyrinth
of no light in which I curl
an endless finger for the cold
to snap. For a lip

to open, I would enter any word
and walk on its tongue. I must live
the moment on a sword, flashing
once inside a life of walls.

Ask any room what it means
to be the space between doors, the sagging breath
of sleep. Ask me
what love can mean that moves
through corridors inside me
and leaks into daylight
through a crack in my skin.

It feels like stopping a bus
where the city ends
and watching a mass transit of souls with no faces
walk along a dry river.

I turn towards a dark bridge,
a brave arm between lives. This place
of arches is the final scene

of my mind. I meet you there.
We dance like smoke against a crimson screen,
the dusk that whispers to the earth, while

heavy music beats the arc,
a spoon clashing in a metal bowl
for more.

The Mexican Laundress

When sunrise throws your shadow, headless,
onto a wall, the Yaquis say
it simply means that day will be
your last. There are no sayings

for shadows that crouch at the base of walls,
locked into their work. This means only
that any day is as another

for a woman facing herself in water,
looking opposite ways like a twisted
card queen, forever tired
in her own reflection.

The water where she seems to pray
is almost rust, so red
with friction of hands and knees.
Soil parts here to let her face

appear through sweat-caked shirts
that splash into her mirror. She rubs
the bones of men

out of linen while the men blow
smoke through their long mustaches
in the silent daylight
of Caretto's Saloon, around maps of Italy

that tell them how alone
their beer and card games make them.
Whoever works with her feet
in one land and her hands
in another

must understand them. She, whose back
bends a cruel bridge for them
to cross with their laundry,

knows how unlovely are the quiet hills,
dry trees and rivers
she will never walk along for rest. Only

her shoulders roll as she thanks the work
for her muscles, fingers dirt
like rosary beads out of folds,
using buttons to count

her sins on and rocks
to count her trials.
Life is no more to her than patting dry
the limp chest of a man

and flapping her hands
to make tortillas in a pause
for breath. The motion never stops.

She sleeps with her hands
making questions of her head; she awakens
bronze pools, pushing
her soulweight onto stone,

pretending shirts. Miles
down the gulch are men
who can feel her palms
forever grinding against their backs.

In the Village

Franz weighed bread on his hand
to remember his mother
who could never feed him enough
to do his work.

His aunt greeted us with a loaf
held to her stomach like a child
she was too old to carry
and pulled her knife through it,
letting more slices fall

than we could eat.
She beat the table
to tell Franz that a son should watch
when his mother has little time,

but Franz had lived too long
in this house to believe
that dying is slowed
by watching.

Animals taught him
more than the professors
he left them for:
to live by instinct,
and a strong heart will advise.

With a Chinese story of the laughing man
who played a drum
at his wife's passing,
Franz would explain the changing

of his village,
how little its people know
and how lucky they are
who have nothing to forget.

The Diary

After four births to a wine-soaked husband,
Grandmother gave up having fathers
for her children. She said that when she died
my mother would know her blood.

Grandmother wrote her times in antique shorthand
with only our names legible
as her script unravelled
when we tried to read it.
She made my mother promise to burn that diary

which refused to speak.
Our only inheritance was her room
packed with beds for visitors,
who rarely came, and cupboards

full with linens she never unwrapped
for fear they would cease to be gifts.
On a narrow path between furniture,
she walked days away;
her life became a needle

stuck in its record while youth
conspired against her.
She bound the veins to her legs and ran
four flights of stairs to buy bread,

which she left always a day to age
before she sucked on it. In the afternoons
she watched the world through her window
until nothing happened,

and she wrote it along the neat miles
of her notebooks.
A drunken priest delivered her to the flames,

her last coins melting in her hand,
as her last daughter saw her father
in the ash of pages
but could not read the smoke.

The Village Painters

I

Vaclav Zak sets animals to dry
when he has eaten all he cannot sell.
The rider by his window

waits for the eyes
Vaclav pulls from his goats
when he is hungry
to see the sky open
and spill its storm

into the kitchen, where Vaclav's wife
takes yards of innards
to the scene of trees and spirits

only a child can dream.
The village burns with his appetite.
While his wife packs membrane,
Vaclav paints a blossom on his door

and another horse
on which to ride away from his knives.

II

Anna Lickova's curtains are the folded fields
she spreads at night
to remember love.
On her floors, a river

leads her back
between the stones she beat her father's shirt against
and the new detergent stacked

behind a painted door, the wood
she throws her hands against,
feeling her way
to the trees.

III

Opening a jug of flowers, Marie Janku
takes sunflower oil from a shelf to thin
her sticky pigment. She snaps
a branch from her plum tree for each color

she needs to fill the space
around her bed.
Her room is a forest, so thick

a blind man would lose his fingers in its walls.
Marie needs leaves
to sleep among, rocks
to answer her
when she calls home the doves,

the red one, the green one, the one speaking
with a man's voice
as she squeezes it out of her fingers.

IV

Lauko, the sausage maker in his second skin,
is the recorder of events
which turn the village year.
On election day, he counts

the drinks his neighbors wash
their votes away with.
When his brother treads cabbage,

Lauko loves his knees
above the barrel rim. A carnival

is when the lightbulb weakens
and in a room too dark for work
Lauko's family sways
to zither music while, at her wheel,

the sister who spins
threads yarn through all the winter hours.

V

Everyone has two dimensions
in Ludmila Prochazkova's eye.
They wear flat clothes in Starkov,
where Ludmila tells how simple
is the long kneading of bread
or hopeful planting
in the sugar beet fields; even
at a wedding, Ludmila
presses the bride's dress and adds
a stitch for every waiting year.

VI

The miners in the hostel won't stop cursing coal
long enough for Christ
to carry his cross out of Stefan Danko's head.
Stefan once drove sheep

to the monastery and prayed
for twenty-six years
before he craved the sound of men

creaking in damp air.
When they dream their own redemption,
Stefan draws

God's face in chalk against the darkness.

VII

The lake behind Zuzana Viragova's face
is older than her smile.
Through water, she remembers

a bouquet and the dark dress
she wore among roses.
The walls she lives between
are thick and buttressed

against the flow of wealth. She cuts
holes in bright wallpaper
to recall the grey moments

which creased her skin
and grew into her hair.

VIII

When she polishes her floor, Cecilie Markova
spits. Her spirit
stands inside her, burning

the cloths Cecilie wraps the dust
from her house inside
and twisting her fingers
so they can hold neither brooms

nor the spoons in her kitchen which stir
the soup she eats alone.
There is a mountain

fallen from a pure world
on which the sins Cecilie rubs
into her furniture are counted.

At every meal she pares the number down.

IX

Natalia Schmidtova sweats until she feels
the sand and stubbled grass
her toes became alive in.
She drinks among the lupines,

sees faces in the yellow suns,
and when she plows
the earth beneath her is a field of stripes,

rows of light
in which she runs

her feet back to their child.

X

Josef Kerak builds people out of wire.
He winds an endless nerve
around the space inside them.
Each of his figures is a fence

walking away from the boundaries
it was made for. Kerak
twists a traveling man

and steps into him to lose
the weight of his own body.

XI

Ludovit's mother has massive hands.
Through all the years she raised him, Ludovit
felt small in her embrace.
He plants another row of bricks

so that his arms grow thick. He wills
his shoulders wide
but cannot fill the doorways
he constructs. His mother

is a pillar of the house
he builds a house around, pitting
the strength of his walls
against her memory.

XII

A train takes Ladislav Garay away
to the stiff collar
at his desk each day. Ladislav files
his eyes among the papers

he is paid to control.
He walks with a straight back in the city,
then hunches at his easel,
pressing his face into the paint
he forms crooked buildings with.
In the portrait of a hero,

Ladislav draws the scars
that grew on his own cheek.
Since the wound, he has not painted

two sides of a face the same.
He eats poor food
while the train carries home his wages.

The Body Washer

Joze the body washer knows each face
he pulls the sheet across. His small town
has one of everything. Furniture died

when the carpenter lost
his footing on a rock.
The ovens have been cold
since the baker passed away, and nobody needs knives
to cut the loaves that have replaced him.
Joze sliced a piece

off the woodcarver's skull,
but the reason for his death
was not in his head. His carvings
were sold to pay
the funeral bills. One night

the butcher failed to see
a drunken car. Years of making sausage
disappeared beneath its wheels,
then a thin-fingered lady

faded in her sleep.
Her daughters never watched her
long enough to learn
how to embroider the blouses the postman's wife

made before the pain
grew tighter in her chest.
Joze bathes friends goodbye
and hoses his affection through the room
where his nights are coffee and formaldehyde.
When the only sound

is a fallen scalpel
on the tiles,
it cuts his recollections short.
He wheels his neighbors past their final door,
helping them the only way he knows.

The Naco We Visit

The edge of a country is its wrong face.
Border towns catch
in the wire, too heavy
with bright souvenirs
to make it across. To walk among colors,

we collect a word
in Spanish from the guard
who waves us through

to enchilada pink
and the rows of little luxuries
that line poor windows.
The exchange rate favors us,

one of our words for a torrent
of theirs, whose town will disappear
when they stop describing it.

In Naco
people bring empty hands to pray
their fathers back
where woven roses lie
above their bones. Small brightnesses

record the good days, cracks
in adobe houses
the bad. We walk the dust

to teach our shoes
a quiet life, the resignation
of a town that will not grow
beyond its cemetery, existing
on the best side of death

and the worst side
of the border.
Where a country offers its eyes

for ours, trains
run out of rails. Families
live in railroad cars,
growing corn in the steps

of passengers who ended their journeys walking.
The wheels they sleep on

roll from one day
to the next, from one side
of a torn name
to the other. In that second town

foreign products are expensive,
the people cheap.
We envy alien spices

and tinted skin
suggesting time in the sun.
As if eating foreign-style
could make us change,
we taste the minutes

of looking at walls
that darken people
as they work behind them.

Promontory

Chinese fingers scratch a tunnel
in the mountain, move inches
every day to let the railroad through.

At night, the little foreigners
bathe alone to wash away
a strange land.
Their job

is placing sticks of noise
that loosen rock and frighten
demons—but not

the desert snakes Piutes say
will eat each Chinaman

and not the avalanche
picking twenty
who will not see the rails kiss
at Promontory

when the photograph is taken,
which has to age
before it shows a yellow face.

Coyote

I will make you small, fold you
into my shoe, and walk
toward your future.
                    You will evaporate,
becoming rain
on the other side, soaking
into the bones of the earth, living
only at night.
              I can erase
your language and scrape
the breath from your lungs
so you answer any question
silently.
          I have drilled a tunnel
through the river and built a ladder
of stars that leans
against the fence.
                  I will conjure
you a life in the trees
and teach you to hide
among the syllables
employers will describe you
with.
    Wear the heat
as a cloak full of holes
when the desert burns
from inside.
              I will slide you
under the border, sell
you to the dollar,
and bribe the clouds
to cover you.
          Soon
you will fit
beneath other men's photographs,
walk in the dark,
                and measure
freedom by the length
of the road before you.

The Sage, Kien-Wu

Kien-Wu's face is a lamp on the mountain
where he lives above mist
and drinks dewdrops from leaves.

Kien-Wu's hands are crossed in his lap
as patient water turns
to frost on his lips.

Kien-Wu is a thread of silk between the clouds.
His clear skin drifts
free of his bones,

which Kien-Wu has left to his friend,
Tse-Khi, so he can carve
them into instruments. Kien-Wu's shins

become two flutes; his skull is cut
and spanned with hide
while his ribs are strung.

Tse-Khi blows through the old man's limbs
as leaves are falling
like eyes on fire.

A Western Businessman in China, 1875

The merchant, Wa Fung, drifts in slow robes
across his many rugs. His wife
shuffles tiny, broken feet

from garden stones to a single stem
in a vase. Her lips
are blood on a powdered mask.
She is a silent ceremony.
By the moon gate

we sip, while prices
rise and fall. Wa Fung
is steam between us.
After tea we explore

the Shanghai streets, where executions
last all day. We pose
beside a criminal's final word.
In the rattan factory, peasants weave
while the butcher is selling human meat
to feed them. In Wa Fung's house,

his daughter is almost a bride.
A servant combs
her endless hair. She clasps
hands deep inside her dress.
Her face is a brilliant scarf,

her husband is silk in the dark.
I float from the wedding
to the lacquered face
of a courtesan

whose small lips eat
the words away from mine.
In a land I cannot change, for one night
I am ice at her side
while the streets burn down to a taper.

Planctus

1. Lament for Marie, the Beguine

Bring black swans from the river.
Marie's heart
has shrunk to an almond,

her eyes
have gone to the light,
the bones have fallen
apart inside her blue skin.
Goldfinch, open your fiery wings.

Empty the whalebone caskets
of their relics. Make room for the milk

from Marie's veins.
Now she is a leaf.
Press her in a book

that she may sleep in golden pages.
Wash her shredded back

and hold her in the palm of one hand.
Wrap her in linen.
Dry your tears and feed
them to doves. Let us ease

her spirit between our fingers
and watch clouds melt
as she passes through them.
When she reaches Heaven,

lepers will step out of their sores.

2. Lament for Hadewijch of Brabant

A black wind sweeps across the thorns
where Hadewijch lies.

Bless the man
who gave her a coat
to die in.

3. Lament for Christina Mirabilis

Lock all the ovens in Liege.
Throw loaves into the Meuse

where Christina
pulls free of her hunger.
Mourn her with shawms

and rattles.
Christina has slipped from her feathers.

Draw her skin through a needle's eye.
Shake sparrows from the trees.
Burn your lilies.

Tie bells to the water wheel.
Chant from the fenceposts
and spin
until you are so thin

your bodies are thread
and the city is a loom. Christina

is a cross of pins.
She is a crumb on the stones.

Tie your arms together
and make a nest on Earth
for every starving pauper.

Haydn's Skull Returning

The old idea was to check the skull
for skid marks
where a melody had raced
out of the brain

seeking the nerve
that led down the spine
and through the tree of blood

into a hand
to write it down.
But the eyeholes were burnt
from long hours at the candle

and the temple worn thin
by the window where it pressed
to let the music out.

Barely cold, the brain
was washed and measured
though it did not answer.
Its house returns

grinning to tell
the other bones how cold
those metal centimeters are

that measure secrets
and how dry air gives the skin
new fingers to hold the cheekbones with.

The Suicide

Such was the suicide's beauty that she was left untouched for fear of disturbing her classical face or supple, floating limbs. She slipped out of her rope, beside the chair, and would not decay. The door was locked, though her fragrance wandered. Unable to resist these arms of rose and incense, I broke into the room to sleep beside her on the floor. We awoke together. As she stood, I pushed my face into my hands, trying to cry her ugliness away.

Marina Tsvetayeva

for Joan Silva

Prologue: A Letter to Marina

In your city of white rain and iron,
I saw death lying calmly
while winter slid
into the gutters. A spirit climbed

from that pale body, scattering flowers
as I almost touched the face.
It was thirty years
since you had listened to the chimes

and saw the birches
bend outside the Kremlin wall
as you lowered your eyes. The prayers
that blossomed on the lips of old women

could have been for you.
Their language
is of a homeless century.
Another country

grew around them
as they knelt to kiss the old one.
Marina, I have not slept
since then but wandered

with your bells in my eyes.
In the churches of expatriates,
I see that almost breathing face
as if it had been your face

of desperate words.
The trees are waking
in a country of their own.
You carried a branch

to other lives. I have carried nothing.
A spirit dressed in lace
has walked beside me.
In our times,
walls are not a home.

We are holding a candle
whose flame rings
a stateless language in our hands.

*

Coming in from the fields,
wearing a dress cut for nobility,
Marina sits in her mother's Polish chair
which has been finely carved
out of hardwood. One hand

gently loosens
a button at her neck
while the other tears
a crust to feed
her peasant half. Marina stands

her ground through revolution
with her rich hand tracing comets
against a changing sky
and her poor hand
buried in her hair,

fingering the fault line
through her mind. She names *outcast*
as her trade
and breaks her only loaf
like cleaving hope.

*

Stretching her money from beets
to potatoes, Marina
plans a meal of soup
and words. She chews the name *Tarusa,*

tipping it from the spoon
into her appetite
for its graves and trees. In Tarusa,

flagellant women ran
themselves into the earth.
They lie beneath the fields
with furrows in their backs.
Marina dances

until her table circles her
and she holds the swirling flavor
of birches on her tongue.
She cannot calm her room. The ceiling

crumbles onto her
in a dream of cold black soil.

    *

Marina reads white poems
to a red audience.
The royal army advances
from her notebook, waist-deep
in Russia. Marina

lifts the poems from the mud
and weeps their losses. These lines
do not retreat. When she cheers
for the Tsar,

her Bolshevik listeners
reach for the hand
that opens so bravely
to catch their applause.
How can uniforms understand

this woman is on fire?

    *

Sergei is away from her.
Marina warms his place
with another man. Each passion
prepares for the next.
Moscow is a huge lover,

too vast in its own sadness
to regret Marina
leaving. The land

falls away like Sergei's arms.
In the condensation
on her carriage window, Marina writes

how faithless
we are to our loves and how true
to ourselves.

*

Marina's cigarettes in Prague
lie awake on a bed of ash
while Marina weaves
a thread of smoke between
the narrow streets.

Her insomniac shoes
tap small hours on the cobblestones,
measuring the lines
she rolls on her tongue, inhaling
words to make

poetry her breath.
She breaks the tension in her lungs
with each new phrase,
and her eyelids cannot fall
between her and these nights

in which the Charles Bridge spans
sleeping water and tired gravestones
leaning against the shadow
of the synagogue. Marina's dawns
reflect the Moskva River

far to the east. She reenters
the room where light cannot follow
and writes alone
that, in a Christian world,
every poet wanders like the Jew.

*

Paris cannot read
Marina. A distant alphabet
shapes her manuscript. She speaks

for a land that fights itself
and will not print
her words. A piece of Russia
has been torn away

and blown to France
where Marina is exiled again
among her own. The only side
Marina claims

is that of the lost.
She swallows the news
of Mayakovsky's suicide
and will not spit his name.
She loves her dear enemy

for the ink
running from his temple.
Marina does not bleed

when opinion cuts her.
She looks to the Judgement Day of words,
when she will bear no guilt.

    *

Marina sinks a hand
into the black mud,
crosses herself with heavy fingers,
and kisses her silver rings
to celebrate the thaw
with Moscow's holy bells.

In France she cannot hold the soil.
She shows an empty palm
to exiles' children,

telling them not to mourn
an Eden they have never seen
and not to give their love
to countries.
All of them are poor.
A thief

had once invaded the room
where Marina served hunger
at every meal.
He emptied his pockets for her.

She carried his desperate coins abroad.
Prague.
Paris.

Back to a land of bells
whose tongues have been cut out.
Marina buys a rope
in Elabuga. In her poorest room,

the weave traps words in her throat.
I say it for her:
Love no country.

Weighing Souls

To measure the weight of a soul, the dying are placed on the scale as flesh divides from the ether. The soulweigher watches the last breath drift away and enters in his book the difference between the live weight and the dead. In afterlife and silence, our departed are mist without conscience. Back in the world, the scale tips at every passing except when exiles die, for they live far from their souls and the border between Heaven and Hell runs through them. They weigh nothing, having left one life already. The weigher of souls weeps as they evaporate. The sleepless vale is never filled.

The Bells

The kremlins of all Russias lie like stolen fruit
on riverbanks. Earth
is wet

beneath them, and sky
is burnt sackcloth behind their golden
roofs. Inside them
corridors run, painted with wild

forest creatures, winding
together at a secret place known only
to the ermine in winter. The kremlins

have walls of solid darkness,
and ovens roar
in their rooms while bells
are cast in the mud, placed far
inside the world to cool,

then hung
among the fir trees
where snow bleeds as it falls.

Sarajevo

Follow the river, where Serbs
are washing their shirts, surrounded
by buzzing trees. When you reach a town
with green and yellow buses

rattling with exhaust
in clouds behind them, overflowing
passengers and staying
loosely to their route, take one
to the hotel on the square

which you will know by the ballroom speakers
playing louder than you can hear.
Sleep.
The rest is a long journey,

and once you reach Sarajevo
the final stretch is a backwards ride
along the stony boulevard

to a street of coppersmiths.
This is the past.
Go underground.
Away from the light

is a sale of carpets, sweets and shade.
When your century catches up with you,
stay in that deep country of silks

while the war goes on above you,
growing slowly obsolete.

The Human Flower

a masque

Introduction

Skin by skin
the human flower unfolds,
peeling from the bones
to which its muscles cling.

Emeralds divide,
releasing the green scent of pine.

Rubies melt,
rusting the land where flags are buried
and poppies grow.

Granite and flint are softening.
Stone disintegrates.
Shards create new shapes for the frame,

the honeycomb,
in any cell of which
a life might bloom.

1.

A man is traveling without a name
to go home to,

without documents to prove
that he exists.

He walks along the faults
on which divisions are drawn

between the shifting plates
of continents whose rulers

never rest. Wealth
has elected itself to office again,

and he whose currency is water
wanders to the edge of all papers.

2.

This mother is a stranger to her land.
Her clothes are wandering
without her through
a crawling mass of smoke
where conversation is conspiracy.
Her child is a shade of grey
in a monochrome country.
She crosses the bridge to infinity,
the dunes of ash
where other creatures seek their young.
She returns as a doe;
her lungs are shadows
and her spine is electricity.
Sparks flash on her tongue
as she licks her child's face.

3.

A refugee from invisible wars
has come to seek asylum
in the antechambers of power.
These walls are torn out of the sky.
Behind closed doors,
dice are rolling. On five sides
each one turns a blank. On the sixth
a name is printed.
The board of directors plays,
waiting for a man with the right name.

4.

The foundry worker has cast himself
new eyes.
They hiss

as they pass through water
to be cooled.
The worker's wrists

hang on springs.
His skull
is glass. The calcium

in his bones
has fused with iron.
He is the machine

too valuable to destroy.

5.

A girl whose soul is yellow
escapes her earthly weight
and faces the endless road
across time.

She is sulphur,
corn and sand,
a flower spraying dust

to her mate. She travels
with no luggage

into the open mouth of the scream.

6.

Having torn the shadow from his skin,
the nameless man

presents himself instead of passports,
cards of membership,

or a certificate
recording his blood group, hair color

and pulse rate, along with details
of the politics to which

he swears allegiance;
but the shadow is a screen of darkness,

and the man's allegiance
is only to himself.

7.

When light has passed
around the mother's shoulders,
profiled her face,
and given her an edge of fire,
she steps away from the pool of shade
with a dark body clinging
to her. Not even light
has a blade so thin
it could sever
the mother from her child.

8.

As if he lives inside a cube,
the prisoner sees walls
in each direction.
He feels for a door,
fingers his reflection,
and kicks at the air.
These walls have no substance.
The prisoner runs
while footsteps breathe behind him
through all his walls,
from each cell to the next.

9.

The man of our times
has iron filings in his blood.
He weeps constant steam

and wrings out his lungs
after every day at the forge, the vat
and the hammers.

He beats himself
until he is a sheet,
then reenters daylight

where he disappears.

10.

Pale dust has drifted across the country,
past the boundaries
where souls disintegrate.
A girl wanders

to retrieve the pieces of herself.
She follows yellow trails
to the edge of sound
then calls out
for a name

that will answer her back.

Epilogue

Finally, the soul must pull away
from the nerves that tie it
to the flesh. Souls
cool as they float toward afterlife
in a landscape cut from ice.

Their voices never disappear.
Certain souls sleep
in the loam while others fade
into the distance, hovering briefly,
then dissolving as a veil

drawn strangely across the world.
Perhaps water turns to lace
or rocks exhale a film of breath.
Elements return

to the crucible, where steam
is the beginning of every story.

Trophy

Somebody wanted him
enough to take a chain saw to his head,
to take the prize
that drove a hunter
into the forest.

He was picked out for his looks,
followed from a distance
because he was spectacular
and his presence
gave life to the trees.

Eating leaves, lowering
his large head to drink, keeping
balance on the buckled ground,
he raised his ears
to catch a sound, and then returned
his attention to the greens,

while out of sight
the eyes that followed him
were smoldering. However clean
the shot, his legs gave way
amid the dizzy foliage and all the sky
was pulled through the centers
of his eyes at once.
The saw buzzed

as it cut the dome
of his skull away
for the antlers to be taken,
leaving behind the jaw and nose, the ears,
a few inches of neck,
and the scent of the few
drops of fuel it used to do its work.

The Bridge

One bridge more, one
   crossing, the new shore,

another set of arches to carry
   us, another language

to learn, a new city, new houses,
   nowhere to go back

to. This is the bridge
   we follow to its end, over

the peak of the road
   where the view circles us

and the sky is ours to fold
   away. We have no papers,

no country. We are running
   on empty, looking

for work. We answer no questions.
   We are nobody's business,

nobody's neighbors. We never
   turn around. After this bridge,

the river is behind us.

Despoblado

I, Diego de Medina, joined
the army with my body
being my one possession. My load
was a sack of amulets
and butcher knives to trade
with natives. His Grace
the Governor climbed
from his velvet saddle
when we reached the north pass
and raised a flag of yellow silk
to please our Lord and claim
the land. An age of silence
ended when we fired a celebration round
and trumpets came alive.
The fish in their streams, the salt
and pastures, became one nation
as we passed north to mercury and iron
through red mountains and onto
a plain that crumbled
beneath us. Our march
crossed the tongue of the sun.
We could not drink our prayers.
Empty space unrolled
with no horizon to cool us.
Our sweat was lost forever.
I saw green in every apparition.
Even the stars were dry.
This was no land of ours
to which we came for gold
only to beg for water.
I clawed the river
while my horse was drowning.
As Rodrigo is the witness
who will sign for me, I swear
this to be true, and may
God bless and preserve him.

Monuments for the Unknown Illegals

For the one who stood on his shanty town hill
to look at the other side,
take a cloud of pollution
and stretch it a thousand miles
to corrode the fence.

For the one who walked in circles
around his own shadow,
hang a shirt on a cholla's thorns.

For the one who earned three dollars
after a day in the dark
assembling goods she cannot afford,
leave a radio tuned
to play her music
in a lantern filled with sound.

For the one whose hands sewed garments
until her fingers cracked,
plant a needle in the earth.

For the one who passed like magic
from the hands of the coyote
into those of the sun,
set fire to a dollar bill
and scatter the ashes wide.

For the one who entered the snow
with his bride in his arms
and came down the mountain without her,
raise a wedding dress among the trees.

For the one whose bones are moonlight
in July, bring a cup of rain
for those who follow to drink from.

For the one who signed his name in spray paint
on the steel contract
placed between the first world
and the third,
erect a monument of treaties
with pages stamped and classified as law,
then let them blow apart
and bless their scattered journeys.

Desert Souls

The cholla glows through an aura of needles,
each with its portion of light
impaled, while the paloverde's soul
turns yellow in its season
and that of the corn is the worm
curled tight in the cob.
Rocks live quietly,

harboring time as solid matter,
waiting patiently for rain
to wear them away.
Storms alone reveal
the inner life of the red formations
when they spark fire in the valleys.
Agave souls grow and flower

briefly, then lean and drift away
from the fleshy blades
that outlive them.
Life and afterlife change places daily
where shadows are draped
across the dunes.
Shafts run deep

into the foothills
where men have mined for souls,
finding nothing
but the ghosts of those who tried before.
Ravens come to earth

and eat the desert's souls
before they have chance to depart.
When a raven is too old
to carry on, a small
black moth is released
from its beak
with an eye on each wing
and a craving for the dust
that colors ocotillo flowers.

Turkey Vulture

The bird of the blood
hangs from the sun
on a rack of bones.
It is never alone
when it rests with shoulders hunched,
looking for an open wound
to receive its penitent head.

Scale

The plates of shadow and luminous rock
that constitute the desert
float above a memory
encased in lava

where the skeletons
of creatures past
are strung together on the fiber
that holds the earth together.
When mountains exhale a long breath

from their caves into the melancholy light
of the universe, the nomadic
insects underground

enjoy the tranquil pleasures
of being small
among the bones of giants.

Learning the Desert

At first, the rocks are an affront
and the cactus serve only
to remind you that shade
is irrelevant. *Nothing here,*
you say, surveying the sweep
of mesquite and prickly pear from one
evaporating horizon
to the other. You look to the sky
as a mirror of the emptiness
before you, but lizards

know better. When they cling to stone,
the heat takes solid form;
and the bats who live in old mines
know by the nectar
that springtime is a scent
made tangible at night. Hawks
have eyes for each ripple
in the light on the desert floor
and snakes know the comfort
of the darkness beneath it.
Don't look

for the trail to lead you home
but study
within a few dry steps
the way the surface breaks
for penstemon to pass through
one petal at a time.

Boat Lane, 1967

Painting the lane at the back of his house is like painting in the dark to the artist who records the scene in order to escape it. He is still young and does not know what it means to take hold of a few houses with the crowns of summer trees above their roofs and make an arrangement of grey, white and brown. He thinks that to paint one must see as a camera sees, and he is afraid to lie. What he doesn't know is that his hand obeys the dreamer inside him who chooses the scene with its lonely lamppost, the upturned bathtub in the yard at the back of the open gate, the rubber tire that is in the picture because nobody has taken it away, and the dreamer sees everything. There is just enough shadow to give form to the walls. Light can only be hinted at in the city where the artist lives, but when he finds the picture again, more than thirty years later, he becomes the dreamer at last. Are the houses still standing? Does the lane still lead to a river? How silently the bricks lie on top of each other. As if they were beautiful.

After Work

The calendar on the office wall
digs in its single claw
and holds on for the night.

The typewriters on their desks lie still
with their teeth in a jar beside them.

Paperweights rest on nests of paper.
Rolls of calculation
lie in the aisles like wood shavings

the clerks leave behind
when they open their umbrellas
and step onto their reflections in the street,

where their minds take on the image
of their bodies
but shining.

Isabelle Eberhardt

Among the slow-burning fantasies
of the occupied zone,
nobody is who they appear to be.

Inhale the lazy scents,
walk across the dunes,
and give up
your body's weight
to the darkness.

Be a friend to the men who lie back
on their illusions,
who float above the ground
with their gaunt faces cracked.

Dress as a stranger
and take fate as your companion
as you measure each dry step

until your thoughts are smoke.
Now you are ready
for the work, the alchemy
of the written word
by which you thread a lifetime

through a moment's eye.

A Cavalier's Wife

An ice-edged cloud the shape of a horse and rider
breaks open the sky above a courtyard
where a woman has been knitting for three centuries,
pausing from her work once every ten years
to look through the gate between its grey towers
and down the cobbled road from which
her husband waved his hat with the yellow plume.
When diplomats step out of their polished limousines,
she does not greet them; neither will she smile
for the tourists who focus their cameras and comment
on the immaculate lace at her wrists and her collar.
Only when the rain sweeps against her face
does she lean back in her chair as if for a kiss.

Writer's Block

The simplest art is dreaming.
Mice come from the underground
to nibble at a fallow note pad.
It helps to be afraid of them,
to stand helpless
as they have their way.
They cannot be stopped, and having stripped
the kitchen they eat the hearts
from books. They arrive
in the hundreds, seeming to multiply
as the night grows long,
until they are sated and leave.
It helps to imagine them as being larger
than they are, to think of them
as being armed, to forgive
them for being hungry and for taking
the perfection from paper. The rest
is instinct. Begin with any word. Nothing
worse can happen now.

A Brief History of Trees

This is the space where the trees stood
before we cut them down to make boats
that would take us to another country
whose trees we cut down to make houses.
Then we grew new trees
so we had wood for our arrows
to shoot at the enemies whose trees
we turned into musical instruments.
We grew more trees
to sell to our friends who had made money
out of theirs, and we bought up all the forests
to make paper, and we cut faster
than the trees could grow. Then we printed
the history of trees
so our descendants could read
about the creatures who lived among them
and about how we feared the dark forests
with their eyes of night and insects
thirsting for blood. It was all
to make room for the sunlight, we say,
and to make the world safe. And we close
with a postscript that admits
it may all have been a mistake, but how
could we have known, when we were strong,
that we would grow bored with music
and forget how to read?

Bach

The flautist at the station stands on the bridge above the trains and plays Bach. He plays Bach because it is slow and pleases the passengers who are tired of always rushing to be somewhere else, somewhere more exciting or just somewhere they promised to be. Whether they wanted to or not, they promised to be at a place where somebody promised to meet them, not knowing how they would need to run to be punctual, and not knowing they would stop to listen to music on the way, music which refuses to be rushed for their sake. They feel obliged not to stop and to keep running so they will catch the next train and not let down the someone who is waiting, anxiously rolling back their cuff to look at the watch that says *late, late*....The Bach is too calm to resist. At any given time the flautist holds the attention of all who cross the bridge and are caught in a net of slow Bach. Just a few bars more, they tell themselves, but the music is old and has lost all sense of time. Every day, they meet obligations and stand to attention. They are faithful, patriotic, unswerving in their sense of duty. Systems will fail without them, financial markets will crash, and they will have only themselves to blame. The flautist takes no responsibility. He plays although he is aware of the consequences. After all, even he has a right to earn a living even though the whole house of cards comes down in a heap and the headlines will name a scapegoat, but he knows there will be Bach among the ruins again tomorrow, and the day after, and the day after that.

Seeing Moscow, 1971

The shadow of our plane moves
like a crucifix
in the clearing between a village
and some birches still
with winter inside them,
brushing past women
absorbed in carrying bundles
from the nineteenth century
to the twentieth in this
glorious fifty-fourth year of revolution.
They don't look up
as we pass over them,
close enough to see
the decorated windows on their homes
and the dark paths they tread in the frost,
but walk in a dream's slow motion
while smoke climbs
from chimneys in delicate threads
cut by scissors of wind.

The road to the city is flat
as the tables in the airport lounge
laden with books for the taking
whose contents are translated
for everyone to read
the texts which keep the country afloat
on a sea of red.
Welcome to Moscow
says the guide
with a military smile
as we look from the bus
at pale flashes of bark
rising in columns
from powdered snow.

From the restaurant window
at Hotel Bukarest,
where we are served our hundred grams of meat,
we digest the view
of a patient line

with pilgrims at the end
of their journey, shifting
in time with their hearts
toward the mausoleum.
Beyond them, the wall and the towers,
gilded domes and crosses
left over from a history
rather forgotten
but too beautiful to destroy.

I wander alone
in my western shoes
down avenues of thunder and steel
with twenty-story walls
staring into space
minus expressions. In little parks
men sit playing chess,
weighing each move
with a statue's gravity.

In a rainswept suburb
a church door opens
and the scent of prayer leaks out.
A body decked in flowers
floats in mid-air. Its face
is waxed for passage
to the afterlife
through a forecourt ringing with voices
from an invisible choir.

Monuments brood
above the traffic: Lenin
with his eternal jaw,
focused eyes, and canyons
chiseled into his coat;
Marx emerging from a stone block
with his left hand frozen
to a book; Mayakovsky
standing on a plinth
with jacket streaming back
from his chest filled with oratory;
the bare-chested worker

whose muscles were cast in a foundry
stepping forward with his wife,
each with a hand in the clouds;
Tolstoy with the worry
smoothed from his brow

and at eye level
the people
who are monuments walking
in grey coats
where their secrets and complaints
are kept warm
as they listen to clocks
that chime
not hours
but years.

Storm Season

Our clocks were set
to time the end
of the drought. Through an open window
we waited to hear July birds
and thunder. The thermometer
showed silence.
                        Then
the sky broke
and rain fell
directly through the earth.

          *

We climbed the summer slope
between green ponds
and apple trees,
listening to crickets in the grass
as water smoothed itself
after leopard frogs jumped in
and, just as lightning first
stabbed into the canyon walls,
a splash of cool air
cut the heat.

          *

The downpour ran its course
and cleaned the air
before the constant
rain that tapped the roof through dreams
of a washed-out trail,
a wrong number dialed,
and a telephone ringing deep in the forest
between the rapid notes
of a rare warbler's call.

          *

At the end of the all-night rain,
we awoke to an arc
of light that spanned
two peaks. What drew us

up the trail between them
was the hermit thrush's song
drawn in brushstroke flourishes
on maple, oak, and ash. Behind Split Rock
we found,
                    set aside for the dark hours
of a smuggler's thirst,
                              four bottles
of *agua* washed clean of their labels
by a flash flood passing through.

      *

Rain upon rain;
with all their blues restored
beside their rusty scales,
the lizards in the sunlight
glowed again.

Some Trains

I

The trains that are pulled by the moon
toward their destinations
pass through towns where the windows are open
and the lamps in the streets
reflect on a skin of freshly fallen rain.
At the speed of a wish
they appear on the horizon
and are gone into darkness
so thick
it turns the rush of metal
into whispers.

II

The trains that have passed through the night
appear at daybreak
as miracles.
Farmers in the misty fields
raise their eyes from the earth
and put down their shovels to wave,
each in his turn,
as a mark of respect
for a deity
long believed to be extinct.

III

The trains that bring bad news
arrive late with no passengers
and cigarette smoke draped
between the racks
the ticket inspectors check
for luggage left behind
with their flashlights scanning each compartment,
more in duty than in hope.

IV

The trains that no one waits for
squeal to a halt in the terminal
where their stillness
seals every exit.

V

The trains that are burdened with memories
make up lost time on the run
with the ease of a dream
repeating itself
mile after mile
night after night.
They hammer the earth as they rush
and stop with such a blow
it spares no one.

VI

The trains that are burnished by dawn
emerge from the longest of nights
to become a cry
whose desperation to be heard
has turned it to steel.

Breaking Down

Everything breaks down in time:
the cassette player
speaks in tongues,
software doesn't function,
and the soul
slips beneath a shadow.
When my online provider stops
providing, I dial
a number that tells me
to dial another
and so on
until I reach a living voice
that speaks with a dusting
of Indian spice
offering me an upgrade
to a more costly version
of frustration. An inspirational
speaker claims
from the television screen
that problems are illusions.
He starts me thinking
about the people whose jobs
left them behind
when they moved overseas,
about the ones who sleep outdoors,
and those whose lives
have broken down
beyond repair. We need to connect
with our inner selves, the speaker
says, to find our way
to the light from which
we emanate. I dial again,
calling long distance
for directions to the source
of life. Please enter your zip code
and date of birth, please turn
inward. If you seek happiness,
don't look around; the world
is broken in places you can't reach.

Praise

In our country, we say *Well done!* We say *Great!* We say *Good job!* We escalate compliments until the language runs out of superlatives. Everyone is doing their best, and we encourage them to do better. There is no room for negativity, no tolerance for making excuses, and the word *doubt* has been removed from the dictionaries. Everybody feels good because we are told we are good. *Superb* is just a starting point on the way toward *fantastic*. The work force is *magnificent*, never veering from duty, and nobody asks for holidays for fear of being demoted to *fine*. The street sweeper's performance is never less than *wonderful*, the doctors are an *inspiration*, and the army is rarely spoken of because words do not exist that adequately convey the grandeur of its presence. Every small achievement must be praised so as to encourage larger achievements, which in turn lead to achievements so *momentous* they set an example for all to follow. The perfectly mowed lawn draws the praise it deserves, the memo worded with precision is framed and hung on the wall, and the placing of a vase in a hotel lobby is discussed with the awe reserved elsewhere for works of art. Everyone is appreciated by law, even my neighbor who has built a gallows in his yard and stands beside it waiting for a comment. The vertical is tall and strong, the horizontal is supported by a beam set at forty-five degrees beneath it, and the wood is planed smooth from the base to the tip. We who live in its shadow wonder whether our street is zoned for a gallows, but we stop to admire it and say how much we appreciate the way the carefully braided rope flows through a slipknot into the noose.

Writing in the Desert

Once you have entered the desert
a lock behind you clicks. A new vocabulary
floods your tongue and leaves you struggling
to pronounce the words. After the first year
you learn that silence is the official language
here. The longer you stay
the shorter the book you came to write becomes
until the manuscript fits on the wings
of a moth. Each dusk, a lifetime's work
draws closer to the flame.

Dry

Dry is the shade of light on a mountain
jutting suddenly from a flat
expanse of desert,
and the ribs in a dead saguaro
are dry as they bend toward the ground
which is so dry it glows.
A cholla stripped of its thorns
is fiber and holes reaching into the dry air
like the hand of a man
who lost his way
and fell through his shadow.
The hooks on a barrel cactus are dry,
as are the spears on the yucca
and the stars growing from the flesh of the senita.
The forecast is for dry,
and when the centipede crawls from the crevice
in a rock, its orange segments
appear as drops of water
walking on a hundred legs.

Late June at the San Pedro River

I

The dove
who landed on a branch at noon
still perches there
at four,

a silhouette against the heat-paled sky.
All that moves

are shadows edging
their way toward dusk
when quail come chattering
from the thirsty grass

and a breath passes through every tree.

II

We look so out of place along the semi-desert road
where meadowlarks fly from mesquite
to mesquite, the three of us:
a man and woman with binoculars slung
around our necks and the small
white dog

pulling her leash to lead
the way with the mountain, San Jose,
to the south of us, the Mules
straight ahead, and the wide Huachuca range
at our backs

as we stride away from the smell
of burning in our car, the latest
failure of technology.

III

Eleven thousand years ago
at this spot
the people killed mammoths,
scraped the bones
and lit their fires beneath a million stars.

When day returned
they looked around at these same peaks
as the gods were waking.

IV

The cactus wren laughs at our broken car.

His voice
rubs against the heat
like sandpaper.

V

I have come to a place of green light where the slow river flows to
wait for the yellow-billed cuckoo. Perhaps the call heard yesterday
downstream will return as solid form and the bird will flash its
plumage against the deeper shades of cottonwood. It is silent here,
except for the dove whose voice is like nature passing from our lives.
Song sparrows peck the water, blue grosbeaks make loops from the
bank, and the day sinks into its bed. For a last time I scan the canopy,
take in a long breath, give it back to the air, and walk away with
silence laid inside me as if an egg.

VI

Night appears first
as the chevron on a nighthawk's wing.
Then the toads
come from the underworld.
And moths—the white,
the grey, the ones with arabesques
inscribed on their wings—
steer a passage
between the stars.

Water Wall

After "La Mer," a video projection by Ange Leccia, in which the tide is filmed from above and projected onto a wall.

I   View from Above

Water crawls toward us
and, slow as breath,
draws away,

approaches, retreats, because the way of tides
is back and forth
as surely

as the way of people
is to attack and possess. The powerful say it is this way
because this is the way it is
with fear and retribution.
They give us this day
our daily fears

until the moon pulls the tide
and the tide stands on edge,
our minds perform

a handstand, the violence
surrenders, and all

it takes is to see
from a different angle.

II   Landscapes of Water

Now it's a Chinese landscape scroll,

now a glacier
without gravity
melting into space,

now a mountain
on the back of a whale,

now a forest
married to rain,

now the light
illuminating the snowflake
inside each drop of water.

III Evolution

In the erotic rise and fall
of muslin waves
the storm in the spray
is white thunder
declaring the aspirations of water
that wants to be air.

IV The Shore

Water brings to land
its depth and its darkness,
the flavor of salt,
and the cold
of infinite distances. Land gives back to water

its flint and its sand,
ashes and rust,
its thirst and crumbled empires.
Water reaches,
land resists;
land speaks in consonants,

water in vowels,
and we come to the shore
for the silence
their language holds inside itself.

V Sacrifice

Here is where mountains go
as they dissolve
when evolution hurries
to catch up with the pace
of industry.
The last refuge
of the rainforest
is the longing
to be tall again
with its head in the clouds.
The desert, once
under water,
goes under once more
with its purple flowers bleached

and its sunsets
washed to grey.
Here are the faces of the gods
tired of telling people
what they wanted to know,
draining from icons
and frescoes
and the altars
on which the sacrifice
was too little too late too burdened
with interest
ever to be repaid.

VI   Memory

The world's memory of itself
is beyond translation
into language; it is the record
of what might have been
had we only recognized
it was addressing us
who could have saved it.

VII   Illusions

These waves could be rumors
of disaster
or messengers riding away
from extinction.
There could be hope in the swell
or the tolling of bells
at the end of the end.

You could be inside a cloud
looking down
or under water
where dreams are the only reality.
It could be dunes you see
shifting with the wind;
it could be a continent washing away.

It could be a veil drawing back,
revealing water
as the soul of time.

Predictions

There will be ice on the moonlight
in the country of wolves
when they rush from the cover
of the trees. There will be dust

on the riverbed
at summer's end, just before
the swallows disappear. There will
be schedules left at bus stops
and old shoes in the road.
There will be blind men

asking directions
and brides dressed in white
selling confessions. There will be a time
of plenty and another

of even more. There will be
a time of need and nobody
will know the difference.
There will be deserts
so beautiful

on the night the cereus bloom
even the lost traveler
will lie down among the thorns
glad to be alive.

Waiting for the Quetzal

Begin in the lowlands, in light
soaked with moisture, where people
are waiting for a bus
they know will arrive because waiting
never fails them. Take the winding road

that peels away into the cordillera
promising never to end.
Relish the view at every switchback
with mountains flowing in and out
of the clouds. Soon it will rain,
the road will turn liquid,
but a mile into the sky

wild avocados grow
and epiphytes take root in the air.
The strangler fig
is water turning to muscle
before your eyes. Listen to the heat

as it drips around you.
Count down the time
to the storm drifting against your brow.
The song of the Nightingale Thrush
makes a bed in your ear

for the cicadas' shrill noise to lie down on.
This is your station
on three feet of earth
that rests on clay
flooding daily
as the forest turns to steam
and back to forest.

There is no light here
except what filters through the trailing greens.
All that remains

is to stare
into the tapestry, pulling apart fibers
and turning back the leaves.

You have imagined the Quetzal so often
it became familiar
before it was real. A sighting

is always too much to hope for
until you bite into the humidity
and the long feathers trail right before you

in the space between stillness
and invisibility.

For Earth Day

Today the rivers flex their muscles
and the heart beneath the ice cap beats
in steady rhythm. Great apes swing
on vines suspended from the sky.
A heron's wings span centuries
and, on the savannah, the shadows
form a sanctuary beneath each spreading tree.
Snow bites into the saddle
of a swaybacked mountain where ferns
grow as light and aspens
lean into the sun. This is the day the whales
heave their massive dreams
through the surface of the ocean,
and this is the night the nectar bats
dust their faces with sweet pollen.
A fox with a spark at the tip of each hair
sprints through the mist in a blue valley,
and the sloth on its bough
in the rain sleeps undisturbed
while we stop the clocks to look
at the world as it could have been.

Twelve Days in Costa Rica

I   The Bus from San Jose

A monk breaks sticky bread
in the bus station café
where he waits with a ticket
to San Isidro while
his companion cradles a guitar
on his lap like a child
who goes wherever he goes.
Plates of rice and something fried
mysteriously guide
travelers to their tables and float
to rest. A television screen
displays a decades-old United States
in silence; another one the soap
dream on a beach whose tide
is washing Spanish syllables ashore.
There is kissing. Tears.
You don't need to hear
the dialogue to understand.
It's romance above our heads
as we board
for the winding winding road
through clouds
to the clouds inside them.

II   Mirador de Quetzales

Kyow kyow the call
repeats four times from deep
forest dark and we walk
on roots to pursue it, climb
where our steps sink
wet into wet
as far as a cypress
with centuries inside it,
as far as the epiphytes
strung between clouds
and the layers of water and leaves
giving way to our weight

when we stop at a new *kyow*
kyow. A quetzal
is close as the rain
drifting slow in the chill,
starting its fine descent
through the trees that part
a second and close
around the moss and ferns
where we wade into darkness
that sings from its core.
A flash in the foliage
of brilliant sheen with a stream
of feathers behind
lands on a bough dripping light
as a squall hits and vision
is washed to the valleys
until trees step out of clouds
and their shadows soak
up moisture as they fall.

III   La Florida

The path to the blue-walled schoolhouse
is lined with bananas and bamboo.
It connects the piercing cry
of a roadside hawk with the green
screeching flock of parakeets, crests
at a basketball hoop circled
by black vultures, and lies quietly
waiting to become invisible
when the hill changes into calls
in the dark, sparkling
from the underside of leaves,
while we sleep suspended in rain
and wake up on a bed
of thunder and bird cries.

IV   On the Road to San Isidro

A driver leaving San Isidro
signals those approaching
to beware ahead.
                    Police?

Fasten seat belts.
               Accident?
Check brakes.
               A sloth
is crawling inchwise
across the road, his patient claws
on the paving and a plea
in his eye where the long hair
parts for the big truck
to wait.
               And it does,
while he pulls himself
to safety at the ancient pace
of mist clearing.

V   The Rara Avis Truck

Each day a truck drives off
the world's edge and arrives
on the route to Rara Avis
struggling to become a road.
The wheels rattle the letters
into all permutations; r-d-o-a,
a-d-r-o, and sometimes stall
at r-r-r-r until the thick tires grip,
water sprays, and the vehicle kicks
forward. A lurch and a growl
place the letters in order at r-o-a-d
as the journey continues.
Spitting mud and bucking
passengers, the wheels progress
to a halt then claw
a few more angry feet
through fresh brown slush
before the motor snarls a protest.
Bridges straighten their spines
in respect when the truck approaches.
After crossing them, it exhales
bad breath and continues
its bitter mission
where even horizontal movement
means defying gravity.

VI   Primary Rainfall

A raindrop hangs on a high-wire
of sound stretched between
strawberry poison dart frogs
with clouds welling behind.
The shaft of light illuminating
a black-faced grosbeak
is snapped by a thunderclap
and the sky blossoms
into a downpour. We hold
to the trail by the soles on our boots,
climb a staircase of water,
then descend with the stream,
parting curtains of rain
to pass through.

VII   Caribbean Rain

Blue crabs' shells
glisten in their burrows
where the noise of the storm
flows into sand
with no difference between
decibels and moisture,
where each wave is louder
than the last, and the rain
is three parts water, one
part thunder, so close
we wipe it from our brows.

VIII   The Bus to San Jose

The radio plays low-volume
songs of romance as we leave
the grey Atlantic tide
for pineapple fields
on two lanes without respite
from the rain. *¡Hola!* Our driver
makes a cell phone call
that lasts for miles, past banana
leaves and misty nests

of oropendolas hanging
from traces of light. Listing
with the angle of the road,
we wind to taller trees and epiphytes,
look down into valleys filled
with cloud and brush,
past ferns and waterfalls, until
city traffic crowds the bus,
still with music's shadow in our ears.

Owl History

I

Emerging from nests of superstition,
owls were the omens
that darkened fields and children's rooms.
Prophecy scattered from beneath
their silent wings
at night when their faces were soft
against the stars. With one eye for wisdom
and one for disaster, they remain
unerring in flight
as they slice into shadows with a claw.

II

The chill in the call of an owl
has crossed entire continents,
bringing comfort to some
while others heard the devil
speaking through a bird
announcing a harvest of ashes
for a stillborn to inherit.

III

Sometimes an owl appears in disguise,
wearing a cowl to pass for a monk. Sometimes a monk
takes off his cowl to reveal
his round face and the feathers
encircling his eyes.

IV

Owls outlived the shamans
who believed their hearing was so acute
they listened to our thoughts. As for those
who ate an owl's eyes
so they could see in the dark,
they walked off the edge of the world
when it was flat.

The Stages of Darkness

The first stage of darkness is the glow
brushed into walls and palm fronds
by the falling sun while mockingbirds fly late
with insects for their taking
as the moon swallows the cool breath
that passes over rooftops.

The second stage is moisture
rising through the soil,
a river of light on the freeway, and the appearance
of a moth on whose wings a map
of the underworld is drawn
just as the scent of the cereus
is layered over that of acacia.

The third is the stage of not knowing
what moves in the grass or what returns
night after night as a call
almost real, and yet so soft
you know it from your dreams, you
who speak only by day.

Dry Heat

We say the heat is dry
to deflect from its burn.
We call uncontrolled expansion
into the desert growth,
suggesting houses are a life form
that flourishes without water.
Words have begun to wear a disguise.
Even the freedom
the president keeps boasting
feels like we've drawn the blank tile
in a Scrabble game
only to find all the words on the board
are already complete.
Homeland Insecurity would better name
the office responsible
for patting us down at the airport,
and every time I hear the city
has a village plan
I look for rural life
but find only herds of cars
grazing at stoplights.
Free-speech zones
make the areas surrounding demonstrations
safe for censorship
while democracy metamorphoses
into five-hundred-dollar
fundraising meals
where the tables are set
with the bones of victims
from foreign policy deployments.
Terror is the key
of the age, repeated often
to inspire love of country
and to foment war,
which is another word for it.
Economics is the science
of loose change trickling down
to a minimum wage
in a working week

with hours based
on a forty-eight-hour day.
English only is the language
of thieves
intent on stealing culture
from illegals who smuggle themselves
across borders
that capital is free to cross
without the Minutemen reporting it.
The rich get richer
in this climate
of a hundred degrees
while the poor rest when they can,
but it's only
dry heat.

Border Sky

The sky above the border changes
by the hour
from the first red streaks
raised by the mourning dove's notes
that pass undocumented
from behind a mountain
to patches of cloud
whispering quiet
as the coyote's steps
as he slips from the grip of first light
into a gap as slim
as his shadow. When the centipede
climbs the dry web
that survives an ocotillo
its segments fill with sunlight
and thirty of its legs
turn into flames. From their overnight roost
come the vultures
to climb invisible columns
and hang all day on the hope
of a carcass
while the blue behind them
becomes bluer. Each needle on saguaro
stems shines like the tip
of a scorpion's tail
when it curls to point the way
along illegal paths
on the way to a noon
that stills hearts.
Swallowtails open and close
their wings like the pages
of a book in which the record
is kept of how colors change
with the onset of thunder
in secret caverns
before a sheet of molten darkness
rolls over the peaks
and the heat clears its throat

to open the border
to all who would pass
by the grace of the rain
that sweeps between countries
and blackens the seam
wound between them.

A Letter to Kafka

Dear Franz, excuse me for writing in daylight;
it's a habit I can't break. I know you have a window
with a view of the stars, but the fact is
I need help. I've developed a phobia to optimists.
Death is entertainment where I live and religion
has become a business. We can see the end
of the world from where we stand, and people just
want a better view. A little darkness
would go a long way, something perhaps from one
of your unfinished stories with injustice as a theme
that would leave us to find a way out.
I need advice. What do I tell a lady I hardly know
who sends a message to say I need to repent
my sins but won't be specific when I ask her which ones?
We get religion knocking on our doors, religion
on bicycles, religion in chains and in leather, and we don't
hear much about blessing the poor these days;
neither is peace very popular. Something is making
people angry; maybe it's that anthem they need
special training to sing, whose notes are a symbol
of what few can reach in this country.
What I always appreciated about you is your sense
of humor, that relentless pursuit of absurdity
that turns out to be the way things are. Perhaps I need
to laugh more. I might make friends with whom to share
a vision of a country deceived into believing
democracy should be run by the wealthy. Living here
feels more and more like being a guest on a game show
where you guess your way to disappointment
and still receive your applause. That's what matters
in the end it seems. Even when you fail to reach
the castle, when you're the hunger artist down
to skin and bone, when you've lost more than you ever had,
been arrested for a crime that never happened
and subsequently declared guilty, guilty, guilty,
there is applause. So this is to say thank you
for the ghetto within, that ramshackle neighborhood
nobody can destroy where everyone has a jackdaw
nesting in their insomniac heart.

The Lost River

Songbirds returning from the tropics
looked for their river
and found a dry bed
where deer stood at dawn
licking stones.
The beavers looked reproachfully

from their dams
and the frogs summoned a final
chorus before deflating
into empty sacks.
The bed was examined
for fingerprints.
Was this the work
of terrorists

or had a gang conspired
to package the river
in waterproof bags
to sell where drought planted fear
on city streets?
Had somebody come in the night
to steal it in buckets?
The moon was called in
for questioning.
It yawned.

Miles of yellow tape
cordoned off the banks,
although skunks sprayed disapproval
and garter snakes
stretched themselves out in the sun
to replicate the shape
of what they'd lost.

The mist turned out its pockets
to show all it had been hiding
were the empty plastic bottles
and rucksacks discarded
by smugglers in the night.
We sent a search party

which brought back a cup
filled with pebbles
and a sack of souvenir reeds.
Photographs of the river
in full flow were circulated door
to door and posted on telegraph poles.
Reports came in

that rivers had been seen, but none
was the equal
of the one we'd lost. Not one
possessed the same delicacy
or bristled with green
broken light.

Maps cracked
along the line that once marked
the river's passage,
and the signposts
that pointed in its direction
leaned over and fell
into the dust.
Politicians feigned remorse

for having ignored security warnings
and tried to make up
by suggesting we replace it
with mirrors
while inside the white church on the desert
the statues wept real tears.
We collected them

in vials to use in our rituals,
stood in line
to raise the effigy of San Xavier
and whisper a prayer
for the river's return. We often go

to look for the painted buntings,
blue grosbeaks and vermilion flycatchers
once common where the river was
and find their reflections

floating like silk handkerchiefs
from a conjurer's sleeve.
Word has it

that a miracle is at hand,
but another word says
once a river has vanished
no magic ever brings it back.

The Doomsday Store

A canister of sunlight rests on a shelf
in a vault beneath the coldest
point on Earth
next to the moths pressed
inside a book whose text
is a postscript to the promised land.
Ice from a diminishing glacier

lies on a bed of stars and velvet
in a box under protection
of a century's darkness.
Here are the seeds of good intentions
and the chemicals that challenged them,
separated finally, and here
is the wire

that once looped around
the tibia of an animal
whose extinction qualified it for a place
in a museum above ground
during the time of plenty. Here are frozen
spores and frozen hearts

locked away in safes with nobody
alive who remembers the combination.
The signposts along the way
leading here are turned
to point back in the direction from which
we come with mementoes

to be stored. Can we get there in time?
Will there be room for the pictures
we took of the birds? Will their tape-recorded
songs survive underground
where everything is stored
ten degrees below
the freezing point of money?

The Invisible Demonstrator

I've chosen today to demonstrate against the war
the way I chose yesterday
to do the same. So I set out walking early
with my dog on her leash and my eyes
turned toward the trees
where I count species of birds. Nobody knows
I do this to protest. When my neighbors pass
and wave, they have no way of knowing
the degree of opposition
I feel toward the government. When I go home,
I wash the dishes to protest, and later
I sweep the floor, and later still prepare my lunch
of protest foods, followed by some time spent
watering the yard to state my opinion
that plants are right and war is wrong.
I'm not interested in compromise. I mean all plants
and all wars. When I clean the windows,
it is to celebrate transparency
and bemoan the layers of deception
that constitute a presidential speech. When I make
the bed, it is more for dreams than the body.
When I lie down to sleep, I know I've done all
I can do for today to stop hostilities.
This is a free country; I can do the same tomorrow—
walk the dog, clean house, smooth the sheets—
and no guardsmen or police will stand
in my way. I'll be polishing the furniture and slicing
bread for peace. I'm determined. There could
be thousands of me gathered in the streets like quiet fire
from which a peaceful light is spreading,
but who would then be home boiling water
for tea? Who would ever take out the trash?

Letter to Wordsworth

Dear William, the first miles north
from Manchester Victoria
ran through a hell of brick and factory smoke.
Trains carried hope to the countryside. By Kendal
I was buoyed by the sight of a clear sky. The local line
to Windermere ran smoothly
through an England that belonged to the world,
not to industry, or so I thought
until I bought the book of your poems at Grasmere
and discovered your horror set in verse
at the prospect of a railway
on your most beloved land. Rash assault, you called it,
and called on us to share the passion of a just disdain.
I'm writing now to share some,
to tell you how the ice is warming and the handshakes
of men securing deals
for oil are colder than ever; how hunters
call it sport when they're the only
side that can win; how advertising tells us
how much more we need and the space to grow it
diminishes as we watch; how forests
are chewed up by machines; how rivers
are stolen from their beds; how yellow monsters without hearts
plough the desert open
until nothing remains of it but the howl and the coo
when foxes and doves nest
in our memories. And I know what would sicken you most
is that so little was done, that so few human beings
would demand that we change, that our laws
would be written in smoke. But just watch, William, how quickly
those in power meet to proclaim there is a crisis.
No, not for the planet, William; only
when their money begins to melt away
do they take action. I suppose, to quote you again,
they are weighing the mischief with the promised gain.

Desert Eyes

We can't focus
after so many years of staring into the sun
on detail close at hand

like a sphinx moth's torso
when it trembles
at the mouth of a blossom that once
we knew the name for

but now exists only
as a scent

which has no edges.

*

Horizons float ahead of us
whichever direction we take, always starting
as a promise
but dissolving long before
we reach them. Then there are new ones

and more beyond them. Roads
don't make an impression.
Distances are measured

in time. The nearest mountain
is a million years away.

*

A kestrel lasts a second
as it sharpens its wings
on a gathering storm.

*

After living near the desert for as long
as we have
we can see sound. To the heat
a cactus wren's call
is a flare from a match
being struck against the sky

and monsoon thunder
appears as toads
like bubbles in the dust.

     *

A layer of the desert peels
away in springtime
when wild colors flow
between its rocks and gullies.
Illusions come later
when we adjust our eyes
to the absence of shadows
and familiarity with the needles
shining from cactus
brings us to see them
as drops of moisture in disguise.

     *

It's so dry
that just pointing
we cut our fingers on the light.

     *

A brief illumination of the desert
follows the sun's disappearance
when every color deepens
and nothing casts a shadow. The centipede

is equal to the fox
and the moth to the owl
in the hours that follow, through which

the moon ticks its way across the sky

and stones turn their cool sides toward it.

     *

Never asking what lies
on the other side of the mountains in a purple line
along the torn edge of the world
from east to west and off into the universe

and trusting neither legend nor mythology
we believe only in whatever we can see
for ourselves:

a scorpion filled with light
skirting the shadow of a rock
where last year's rain
pooled in a hollow.

     *

The light of our imagination reaches
into crevices where rock
has a pulse

and bronze
shines on a lizard's neck
as he licks up drops of darkness.

     *

The weight of desert on the eye
is less than that of a dragonfly on water
when its wings are as transparent
as a mountain in the sun
and its reflection
winks before it disappears

in the time it takes for a storm cloud
to fill an arroyo
with red flowing mud.

     *

Here are the tracks that ask
to be followed, into the lives of the coyote
or javelina. They lead

through the ruins of fallen saguaro and across
a dry stream bed. When we do follow them

to their end, we see everything again
but through the eyes of the wild.

The Devil's Sonata

A stirring in the universe
suggests a theme. Cicadas have rosined their torsos
and keep all the world awake

except for a violinist
who dreams in sound. He lies
on a mattress stuffed with melodies

beside an unfinished letter to a friend
for whom the stars
are nails that hold the sky together,

yet something loosens
in the woven darkness. A melody
comes through the open window as gently

as a thief and flows through the room,
accessible only
to the dreamer, who luxuriates

in phrasing that sparkles in his mind
but turns to dust
when he wakes. He knows someone was here

playing with long fingers
on an instrument with light for strings,
and as virtuosity comes without practice to the Devil,

the signature is obvious. Now the work begins:
claiming his music
by writing notes in mortal time.

Cheap Mangos

There's an easy flow of music through
the speakers at the supermercado
where papayas ripen while you watch
their skins disintegrate
the way a man's skin does
when he's found on his back in the desert
facing the sun with his mouth locked
between a scream and a prayer. His trouser leg
is torn where a coyote
came to gnaw at his thigh
and of his right forearm only
the bones remain, while on his left wrist
a watch still measures time.
The music has a teardrop in its beat
and nostalgia in the singer's voice
but the juice aisle is a happy place
with any flavor you'd remember
from a trip across the border
going south to a colorful village
with peppers stacked in the market
just like these red, green, yellow ones
displayed in the order of their bite,
a village likely similar
to one the woman left
whose sweater clings to what remains
of her where she collapsed
in a pair of sports shoes good for many
more miles with the tread on their soles
and Just Do It style. Something pulled at her hair
where her scalp peeled away
but the strap on her brassiere
is indestructible as the belt
that falls slack where the flesh has wasted
from her hips. Had she made it
to a road she might have found
her way to Phoenix, to the store
where the cakes in the cold case
are churrigueresque and mangos
are two for ninety-nine cents.

The Deep Frozen Desert

Beneath the ice light of the northern sky
in a mountain six hundred miles
from the nearest tree
where frost runs deep into stone
and the only star is a signal
from a disappeared world

the seeds of a desert go along
the blue tunnel for storage
in a vault where they wait
for springtime to flower
from snowdrift and memory.
Here is mesquite and a crystal
of cold to preserve it; here

are prickly pear and sage
held in trust for the day
when the sun reappears; here
are agave and ironwood labeled
with ink that glows in the dark
like each golden segment
in the scorpion's tail

and the hourglass of fire
on the spider who crawls
between the stacks
of silver packages bearing
the indestructible seal
of night-blooming hope.

The Bat God

With wings of silk and a velvet mask
he hangs in a recess
until the dark is thick enough to stir

then the blood flows faster
to his ears
and they open to receive the music
made by stars. He's a memory

that can't find a way
back into the mind. Imagine a wolf's heart

shrunken to fit
inside a tiny breast; imagine
a flame as a tooth. When you wake up
in the small hours

thirsty for light
and reach for the switch he'll be there;
he'll be silence

with an edge so sharp
it cuts. Imagine navigating
fear with a map you can touch
but not see; imagine

your reflection flying
from the mirror

and never coming back.

Mining the Sky

First they came for souls
and then for gold;
later it was copper
when the tracks were laid
to carry it down
from where forests grow
into the sky. They came
with mules
to bear their weight
while they blasted secrets
the mountains had kept
to themselves
through millennia
while the desert
lowlands were too wide
for anything but birds
to cross and they saw
hummingbirds each time
they crawled out of
the darkness. They spoke
with hammers and drills
to forge themselves a language
all could understand
wherever they were from.
They arrived with a thirst
and slaked it with water
until it turned to madness
which they slaked
with whiskey.
They came
without intending
to remain; they took
and took and gave back nothing
when they left.
And their appetites
survive them
like the rust that eats
the machines
they left behind.

RECENT

Sense of Place

A place is somewhere we get used to,
some oaks and juniper
with Mexican jays and bridled titmice
flashing in and out of view
and turkey vultures holding
in a circle overhead until
the light calls them down as it fades.
There's a road that pretends

the town that used to be
still is, a creek with water sometimes
and a bed of silence
at summer's height and a peak
to look up at while walking nowhere
in particular. It's hard to tell

exactly where a place begins: at the mailboxes
behind the sign bearing its name? where
the familiar sycamores jut
up against the hill slope on the way in?
on the red dirt mile that leads
there from the north? at the first
acorn woodpecker's cry?
More animals than people live there;

they clamber on the roof at night,
come silently for water
at darkness' edge, crowd into the narrow box
set for them on a pole
and leave it for the moonlight
every night. We never know a place

for what it is until
we see it through a two-inch slot
that opens to the world or from
the spaces no one ever uses
but the rattlesnake
who stays in her one place and waits
for everything she needs to come to her.

Traveling East, Then South

A river of dust
flows under the bridge
at Exit 306
where the road swings toward
the billboards pasted
on the southern sky
telling all who pass
The Thing is near
and steers its way
between sparse vegetation
on the winter glow
draped over cold
desert hills. A few clouds snag
on the peaks to the north
while the rest of the arc
across the world is blue
with yucca leaning
on the chill
and shadows slipping
into sunken beds
that cut a crooked course
beneath the eye
of a hawk on a telegraph pole.
Sunlight crackles
in the pecan groves
where branches cannot hold
its warmth. The rocks
rising to the east
are the shape of time.
After the turn south
a solitary
western meadowlark
holds a breath of a stem
just high enough
to grant an unobstructed view
beyond the grasses
toward the distant shades
in jagged greys.

Silence

The fire burned down in the stove
and a silence descended

around us while we slept.
It occupied each frozen limb, spread

evenly across the ground,
and even Silver Peak became

a whisper in the forest's ear.
Two deer

came to listen
to the buried language

from the time before
the animals were named.

A Canyon View

At the entrance to the canyon, grass
turns to stone and scales the low clouds
in the cowboy sky. There's a hundred-year-old
scent of gun smoke in the air,
the morning rain evaporated
from the stones on which it fell
like ink on a government treaty,
and the echo from a miner's pick
ricochets from wall to red-rock wall,
all the way up to where the peaks
swagger in sunlight, and pines
sway back and forth in the Apache wind.

The Descent

The vultures ride
on carrion scent
through the day's penultimate glow.
They are a vision
of souls holding on
to the light
with their primaries frayed
and they tilt gently earthward
as the earth rises
to meet them
with blood on its breath.
Asleep on the wing
they pass from the sun
to the stars
in a silence
picked clean as a bone.

Black Flight

When the forest has turned into dark scents
on a bed of needles and leaves

with insect voices as the night's continuo

the bats become
a long silk scarf pulled between the fingers of the trees.

Dismantling the Town

The first decision is whether to close
the jail before the bank or
let everybody go and take your chances.
Grocery stores are next, leaving
a few grace days for the saloons.
Sweep the floor of the barber shop
and break its mirror. Distribute
the final letters to reach
the post office and send the unclaimed ones
back on the last stagecoach.
Cut down the hanging tree.
Take the bunks out of the brothels
and leave them by the creek
for the birds to take whatever they can use
from the stuffing for nests
come spring. Pull up the floorboards
from each house, but leave
the rattlesnakes beneath them alone.
Give back to the earth
its adobe bricks and tools
that will rust away
to nothing. Leave Main Street
where it is to run its course
from the creek bridge to the bend
in a road with nowhere to go.
Haul away the walls, roofs,
window frames, and doors. Load a wagon
with spades and copper kettles.
Feed the mules well. By sunset
they will be out of memory's range.

Biometrics in the Desert

We who entered the desert
never asked for the ocotillo's permission,
never requested application permits
from the cactus wrens,
never had papers issued
by the summer rains, never registered
with the saguaro, never stood to attention
when listening to the mourning doves call,
never left our fingerprints on file
with the garter snake, never pledged allegiance
to the sacred datura, never learned
the official language of the sphinx moth,
but we offer up our biometric souls
to the flower
of a cereus that blooms one night
and lets us disappear
when light returns.

One Look

A black vulture touches the edge of its range
with a wingtip, turns in sunlight
and steers itself away
to new territory, with a wrinkled face
looking down
onto the brittle grass and cracked
old trees beneath, where a long snake
is absorbing warmth in mid-
November, curled across a path as live
calligraphy shifting
from dust to undergrowth
as soon as someone comes
too close, and it slides through the eye
of their imagination
when it disappears into a tangle of darkness.
In this tiny corner of the universe
we are given one look
before the earth takes back
what has been revealed to us, absorbs
it in the glassy blue at noon
or drinks it down
with a swallow six feet long
while we look the other way for one
melancholy second
and on returning our attention
see the last gilded scale slip
into a world with no sky.

Line Breaks

In memoriam Gayle Elen Harvey

Whoever lives by the line
knows how to take a switchback turn to reach
the meaning

promised in the phrases
that carry one thought into another until
there is light in the language.
Each word

is ordinary before
the one that follows
transforms it.
Paper

could be snow
falling by the ream, or apples
become the scent of rain; always there is

an element of surprise
transforming what we think to the gold

the alchemist long dreamed of
but finding lead
would always be lead
gave up his kitchen to the poet

who knew better
how to stretch the words we use routinely

across the page
until they are luminous.

The Lost Teacher

Where the wind cut low across the treeless
hills with their edges of stone,
Mister Shaw took his paints
to mix with earth he scooped bare-handed
so he'd have more than the color
on the canvas. His job
was teaching us to draw, but he showed
us his landscapes so we saw
that something more than lines
matters in art. There were the sodden
inclines, the cloud-tinted curves
and tors jutting into what light
the sky could spare, and there was the haunted rain.
The draftsmanship needed
to depict such a place
couldn't be taught. After the uphill slog
to reach the right view, all was guesswork
as to where, beneath the stubborn grass,
to find the bones.

Melancholia

My street on a bright afternoon
with its foraging doves
in one hundred and six
degrees of stillness
has an atmosphere of waiting
for something final
to happen, like a set
from the film about one way
the world could end.

Would we know by the grackles
refusing to roost at dusk
and circling into
the oncoming night, or by the hush
when people stop arguing
over evil and good
or who is to blame
for the shortness of time?

It is quiet enough to hear
debts being forgiven
and the interest rate falling.
There's an amnesty
for everyone who crossed the border
without asking permission.
It reminds me of the times
the power was cut

and people took chairs
onto their lawns
in solidarity with the heat
when the moon was a bead of sweat
on the sky. If that were the way
it had to be, all at once, with nothing
to do to but accept
our fate, we could all

be homeless and wealthy and desperate
in the last blink
of Earth's eye. But the end
is a drip, not a flood; it comes

to one species of bird, to a jaguar, to
a flower no one knows about
until scientists declare
it dead. It is approaching

too slowly to make the news,
and it isn't a film. It happens
while we're looking away.

Freefall

Between the desert and infinity
the sky shifts from blue to black
while a weightless glow
rises from red earth and thorns
through air becoming purer
until it thins beyond breath's altitude.
Mountains fall away, rivers tremble,
grasslands are burn marks made by light.

It's so cold, the seasons
don't come this high, and the planet
swings from the stillness here
with its gentle weight in balance.
Already the air is too weak
for living in, and helium
climbs above time.

With a continent spreading below,
and dark without end above,
the journey continues its vertical course
to where it comes into view
that we're living in a layer
the thickness of a leaf
in space beyond measuring.

This is where the checklist begins: remember
oceans with salt on their tongues,
forests with wings
negotiating narrow space,
plains billowing when a cloud
casts a shadow over them,
and canyons where a voice

is never released from its echo.
Now the door opens. Remember
the lizard with lightning
for a spine, the fox
who burns in the snow, and the whale
upon whom all waters

eventually wash. Twenty-four miles above
the Mescalero Escarpment, the next step
leaves no footprint. The earth rushes
at the speed of life into the unfiltered glare
of the sun.

Afternoon Walk

The sky is edged with thunder.
We're in shadow
one minute, all alight
the next. Houses pass at walking pace

until the street ends
at Grand Avenue, beneath
the billboards and evaporative coolers
that rise above the industrial roofline.
Pigeons on a wire

scatter into sudden flight
when a red-tailed hawk glides
through a gap between the clouds.
The sorry shell

of a donut shop
standing empty on McDowell
is a cube of daytime darkness
contained in glass
where the wind comes from the west

to pry its weakening frame
apart. Here comes a man
so tall he has to bend
to say *hello,*

another shouting
at his off-leash dog,
and a fresh gust
that meets us head-on
and homeless at the corner

of 3rd Avenue
where a synagogue turned pawn shop
stands firm against all weather.

The Factory

I

When they laid the first brick they said,
This is progress,
and then they laid another, promising to carry on
until there was a wall
where previously the wind had blown without obstruction
across the grass. The wall
was high and strong, with just one row of narrow
windows for light to pass through.
Look at what is possible, they said
as they drew up plans for the second wall.
These will stand through any storms, they claimed,
and storms came to test them
and the walls remained.
Foxes came to sniff. They didn't understand
what was happening. Swallows
flew above and in between the walls
until the third and fourth sides of a mighty rectangle
were complete. Sometimes a swallow
would go in through a window and fly playfully
out of the open space held aloft
by the walls. *This is the future,* they said.
This is the place
where darkness will turn to money.
So they covered the space with a roof
which blocked out light
except for the long, dusty shafts
that streamed in when the sun
was on the window side, and the valley appeared
to sit deeper in the earth
because of the weight
pushing down. Only a circling hawk
remained of the sky. They raised a tall chimney
and fed it with coal. *This is the power,* they said,
that nature forgot, and as they bowed their heads
in prayer, a viper
slithered by and spat a hiss.

II

Many came to see it. Many more
entered by the door and stayed inside until each day
was over. Those who praised it
never went inside, but said to those who did,
You're fortunate, be grateful. So the line formed
every morning, and each man
bowed his head as he moved to his assigned position,
while outside the deer
on their way to the river ran by
until water no longer ran there
because it had been redirected,
and after it had been used
it became a kind of poison,
so the decision was made
to have it soak into the ground and disappear,
but it was still there
like fire just beneath the surface of the earth.

III

We need another one just like it,
they said, and they marked the ground
for the new one to stand on. *We must cut down
these trees,* they said, *and lay a new foundation
that will seal the earth.*
It looked just like the one before it,
and those who entered looked
just like the ones who entered the first one.
Two were not enough.
However many they built,
they kept on finding people to feed into them,
and the many chimneys
poured waste into the sky
as if to make an offering to whichever gods
survived in the smoke.

IV

So it continued, each one followed by the next,
until no trace remained
of the grass in the valley and the trees on the hills,
and nobody who came to see
what had replaced them
could ever imagine the way it used to be
when the air was clear enough
for the sparrows to be seen
with their feathers turning gold
as they flocked in early sun.
Don't think about the past,
they said, *your memories will not feed you.*
And they kept on building,
beating down the earth
to make it level for another floor,
creating enclosures where once had been space;
and when they were sure
nobody could remember what they had replaced,
a man old enough to have been dead several times
stood up to speak about what had been lost,
but he could not be heard
above the growling of machines.

V

More, they said, *we need more.*
And it did not matter how many,
they were too few. Some sparrows appeared,
and a lost fox, but no matter
how few were the animals,
they said, *They are too many.*

Undocumented Land

Nothing but bones remain

where the desert floats
toward the sun

of a man who lost his way
between countries

and left a femur like a hyphen

from the punctuation that survived
the text of his story

about stopping where directions

intersect to make his choice
of which to take. A tibia

points toward a scapula

scraped clean by the light
next to a mandible

biting into the ground

where a comma would be placed
in a sentence

expecting it to be continued.

The Unfinished Earth

Homage to Cézanne

The horizon just trails off without a single line
to define it, the middle ground
is cross-hatched green, and color is an echo
in the blunt–shaped rocks. As if

creation hadn't reached us. As if it all
could still change course
with the fires underground emerging
where oceans came to be
and forests woven into a mesh

too dense for anyone to penetrate
except the fox
and the night air. There would be quarries

with pines chipped out of them, ravines
dry enough to crack open
for the darkest rivers to carry their own reflections
out into the light. Take it apart,

put it back together
with more weight in the shadows
than in the mountains casting them. There's breath

in every white space
where the universe is speaking, and patience
flowing through the valleys,
while the grass thinks about what else
it could be. The slightest gestures

reveal the most: a pencil
trembling between the first stars,
a tree

drawn by a man
with one eye inside the landscape.

Lynx

A cat with one paw in the night
moves slowly on a dirt path
where the sun expires
into a cool skin of light
left behind with each step.
He alone sees what he sees,
and he is alone
where the ground gives beneath
his easy weight. His sudden face
parts grasses and his feet
soften stone when he stands
looking down at his reflection
in shallow water pooled
in a hollow. He can move
as fast as a guess disappearing
in trees or be frozen so still
that his heart stalls
while the blood beneath his fur
keeps flowing. There he goes,
down a path into a thicket, with a spine
that dips between his shoulders
and his tail and a flowing stride
that hides the tension
in his web of nerves.

Sky Island Encounters

Once there was a turkey strutting
down the path, and once
a golden snake
stretching long to soak up warmth;
once a deer

stopped suddenly in time
when we were in that moment;
and once a bear
passed along the far edge
of a stream
on his way to the saddle where ferns

make lace of the light.
Once a lizard
turned to amethyst before us,
and once the ground

swelled with toads that bubbled
through the dust.
A fox once

leapt out of the moon
and sat on the road.
We saw them all. They did not stay
but turned for wherever
they needed to go

as the ocelot did
who lived here
once.

The Path

I would walk that path only so far, never to the end,
because I didn't want to kill the mystery.
                                        —Gary Fry

Knowing extends only to the first
tracks the deer leave
along the path that goes where its own mind
leads. Give or take a shadow,

nothing falls
across it. It gives back each step
you make, following
the threads of light that hang
from the trees. The downy woodpecker

has seen where it ends,
and so have the raccoons
whose noses pull them through the night.
If paths could believe,

this one would be agnostic,
leaving anything possible
while denying there is one true way

anywhere. There's a rise and a dip
before the bend, then

the forest claims possession
of the narrowing
as it holds to the slope
with a bobcat's claw, lifts itself
on the wing of a Cooper's hawk,

and sees everything around it
with the never-closing
eye of a fox.

Trains at Rest

The old ones feed in peace,
remembering their predecessors
who wandered back and forth
between the same two points
and died for lack of imagination.
They still look up
when a long freight rumbling
makes them think about the past
when they escaped to other continents
and discovered the edge of the world.
Some were captured
and condemned to black air
while others ran beside rivers,
over mountain passes,
and in dales whose stillness bowed
at their passing. They became
so familiar it was thought
they were tame, until nighttime
when they called out
from deep inside themselves
as only the wild can do.
Those who breathed fire
retired with bad lungs,
and those with romantic names
aged before their time,
while the least fortunate
were those forced to carry the innocent
away to where no one would find them
and who retreated in shame,
but on holidays they receive
a few loyal visitors who come
to forgive and to offer them
each a handful of coal.

Mozart at the Hanging

The first time, he was just a boy visiting Paris
when his father took him to see
how it happened. It was pure
theater: the crowd assembled for a spectacle
and the stage
raised high for all to see.
As a grown man, he lived

close enough to the *Graben,* where Viennese hangings
occurred, to be ready whenever
the time came around,
and he skipped down the stairs in a hurry
so as not to miss the moment
the audience had come for, many of whom
arrived with a tune from his latest opera
running through their festive minds.
He'd have looked like one of them

with his tousled hair
and an eager smile, straining
for a better look, made taller by the tension
when he raised his heels
and felt the muscles tighten
in his calves.

Without a Net

...and gravity
Gets every one of us eventually; what matters
Is the beauty we can do, our balance
Before we meet the ground.
("Once, We Were the Wallendas" by Don Haynie)

You can walk on air
or a two-inch wire spanned across the heat
to show the land beneath you
perfect balance.
                  From one red rim
to the other, in the company of ravens,
with concentration for a safety net
and a view that cuts into the earth,
is a straight line that sags a little
where you tread.
                  The canyon walls
watch every step. The river below
dashes itself against rocks,
gathers itself together, and asks
whether you can do that.
                        All that holds you
is a cloven-footed pact with the forces
of chance as you lick
the taste of falling from your lips
and become the center
of attention.
                  The crossing takes years
while the seasons rotate around you,
through forest fire to ice,
with everyone wanting to know
if the other side
                  will still be there
when you reach it.

My Starling

One Sunday afternoon he fell from the sky
(or maybe a stunted palm)
as a couple walking past
stopped to look at the handful of feathers
and twisted neck

the way we watch the Syrian war on television
without knowing how to help.
After they moved along

I went outside to bring the bird
in from the hot asphalt
and place him in a carrier,
thinking he would quietly expire
even though we fed him
through a tube, and later with tweezers,
as a parent.

Within days he stood up straight
and the elegance emerged
of the long beak extending
from the skull. Starlings
come in hundreds, thousands,

in the winter when they line
the telegraph wires for miles, but one alone
seemed worthy of a name
and of a home. So he stayed
and began to sing.

We heard this week
ninety-three thousand have been killed
in Syria. No names for them
as they rise in a black murmuration of souls.

The Wall Between

This is the wall that was built to keep the jaguars out.
It's too high for them to jump over
and too long
for them to walk around.
The senators all made speeches

about the danger in having jaguars roam
wherever they want. We could be in our backyards
or taking a walk when one of them
approaches with a fire
in each eye. They move so quietly

that nobody should trust them. Most of the speeches began
with *Now more than ever* and went on
to say *We must draw a line in the sand*
which the jaguars cannot cross. And the jaguars
grow thin and weak

from pacing up and down along the wall,
sniffing and pawing the ground
to feel for a way through. Despite
being told what a threat they impose
when we go the wall in the night,

we can hear from their terrible cries
that all they want
is to live.

Drought in the City

We watch every day for a sign
that points to rain. Last week, a hawk
out of its range flew low
over our roof, and then a headache
blew across the room. What is happening,
we wondered, when an oriole
came today to the juniper across the street,
which no oriole before
had ever found. A lost night's sleep
sits on the bed, while the sun's pride
swells to bursting point. The sky
to the north is gunmetal grey,
and dust to the south
has turned yellow. The orange tree
beside the house gave one
last call to Earth and died
with a crack in each of its leaves.
But the finches and doves still assemble
at dawn, the geckos come out
on the front porch at night,
and you would think from the water
sprayed onto our lawns
all is well. We have crawled
to the mirage and learned
that illusions suffice
in the absence of rain.

Clear Sight

Take a few steps into wilderness
and you forget
all the passwords to your online accounts.
Here are the earth's foundations
pushing through the surface

while thoughts of the financial index
are eclipsed by those concerning
the latest numbers for goshawks. When you reach

the stream where a dipper stands
on a rock, your habit
of checking your pocket for the house keys
has been finally broken,

and at the rough edge of the world
you see what the wolf sees,
surrounded by land as wild as he is.
The record of his existence

is a trail of bones left behind
and the cloud of breath
wrapped around his call

when he is still and alert
to every shiver in the grass.

The Man Next Door

The neighbor who wants to know everything
has a way of asking, even though
it's none of his business. But he seems harmless,
so you tell him where you're going, why
the next house along has been empty for a week,
and put it down to friendly conversation.
You're aware that he's watching

you leave and come home, not that it matters
any more than being recorded
wherever you go, by a camera that sees
each withdrawal and deposit, by one
placed in the stairway where you work
and one above the swing
in the playground at the park.
Why should you care?
If you've done nothing wrong
there's no need to worry.
It's all to keep you safe,

even if safety is a state of mind
when the camera doesn't stop
bad things from happening
but just records them when they do.
Where can you go to snuggle in peace,

let alone have a discreet affair?
How wrong is wrong enough for consequences?
The cameras never sleep. Do you? Do you know
who the four thousand in Lower Manhattan
are focused on? You get facial recognition
thrown in for no charge.
How far apart are your eyes?
How broad is your nose?
Who does the measuring?
If you need to feel secure,

install your own system
with a dummy for only fifteen bucks,
positioned to intimidate.

If you've done nothing wrong
there's no need to worry.

China installed ten million cameras in a single year.
London has one for every thirty-two people.
Chicago has ten thousand recording
the income gap between the rich and the poor.
These cameras announce a place is safe for investmen⁻,
a nice place to shop
and buy more than you need.
Even if someone is watching, keeping count,

nobody will stop you
before you spend too much,
and when the man next door asks
how much your purchase cost,
you can never be sure whether he knows already.

Poem for the Beginning of Time

I

   ...had preceded the moment. In
the absence of gods it fell
to chance and darkness; there was
no plan, no where. And the distance
came close, and it opened, and
water reached for shores to contain it.

II

Against a backdrop of many-colored nebulae,
rocks without mercy collide,
and from the cacophony, through a luminous
blue, a dacnis flies
with its red eye and scarlet thighs
glowing and a song
repeating a note determined
to last beyond the crash
beating itself
into silence.

III

Dust had nowhere to settle.
The motes floated, each with its own
little sparkle and hue. They comprised
a continent in anticipation
of its planet.

IV

Caribou follow by instinct
a route across space
yet unmarked. Plovers
in all their varieties from golden
to snowy, are drawn by a force
stronger than light.
     The trails
for migration are already marked,
waiting for land to form around them.

V

*In the wake of an ice-white flash
came stillness;*
           *in the wake
of the stillness, the grinding began
from which mountains
emerged.*

VI

Between snowlight and starlight,
wolves race to a world
where the rain

already falls on the snail,
and the whale

in the water calls
out to the places language
cannot reach.

VII

*Through the fires erupting and ocean beds
buckling, the frost on the backs
of massive creatures who wandered
until the ground opened beneath them,
and the coming of the margay, ocelot, osprey
and kite, there were prophets
who said that...*

Acknowledgments

Poems appeared as indicated in the following books and chapbooks:

No Man's Land (Brushfire, 1983): "In the Village," "The Mexican Laundress"

Old Water (Brushfire, 1985): "The Diary"

Without Shoes (American Studies Press, 1987): "Promontory," "The Naco We Visit"

The Village Painters (Adastra Press, 1990): "The Village Painters"

Measuring Time (Trout Creek Press, 1990): "The Body Washer"

Wear This Country as a Stolen Coat (Brushfire, 1992): "Coyote," "Despoblado"

Forget the Country You Came From (Singular Street Press, 1992): "Planctus," "Haydn's Skull Returning," "The Bells"

Straw Bones (Beginner's Mind, 1992): "The Sage, Kien-Wu"

The Human Flower (Trout Creek Press, 1993): "The Human Flower"

The Insomniacs (Slipstream, 1994): "The Bridge"

Outposts (Taxus Press, UK, 1994): "The Suicide," "Marina Tsvetayeva," "Weighing Souls," "Sarajevo"

Country of Two Seasons (Pudding House, 1997): "Trophy"

Assimilation (Main Street Rag Publishing Company, 2000): "Monuments for the Unknown Illegals," "Desert Souls"

Common Sightings (Palanquin Press, 2001): "Turkey Vulture," "Scale"

A Normal Day Amazes Us (Kings Estate Press, 2003): "Learning the Desert," "Boat Lane, 1967," "Isabelle Eberhardt," "A Brief History of Trees"

Return to Waking Life (Main Street Rag Publishing Company, 2004): "Seeing Moscow, 1971," "Storm Season"

Places You Can't Reach (Pudding House, 2006): "Bach," "Breaking Down," "Praise"

Waiting for the Quetzal (March Street Press, 2006): "Late June at the San Pedro River," "Predictions," "Water Wall," "Waiting for the Quetzal"

The Porous Desert (FutureCycle Press, 2007): "Writing in the Desert," "Dry"

The Dreaming House (Chippens—online, 2008): "The Stages of Darkness"

Dry Heat (Origami Condom—online, 2008): "Dry Heat," "For Earth Day"

The Interior (Island Hills Books—online, 2008): "Twelve Days in Costa Rica"

Melancholy's Architecture (Slow Trains—online, 2008): "Some Trains," "Owl History"

The Epistemological Question Mark (March Street Press, 2008—extended
    version of 1994 original): "A Western Businessman in China, 1875"
The Lost River (Rain Mountain Press, 2008): "The Lost River," "A Letter
    to Kafka," "The Doomsday Store"
From the Age of Miracles (Slipstream, 2009): "The Invisible
    Demonstrator," "Letter to Wordsworth"
Border Sky (Brushfire, 2011): "Border Sky," "Desert Eyes"
The Devil's Sonata (FutureCycle Press, 2012): "The Devil's Sonata,"
    "Cheap Mangos," "The Deep Frozen Desert," "The Bat God"
The Chiricahuas (Seven Circle Press—online, 2013): "Mining the Sky"

"After Work" appeared as a bookmark from Scottsdale Cultural
    Council.

New and previously uncollected poems appeared in the following:

Abbey: "Line Breaks"
Atlanta Review: "The Descent"
Canary: "Lynx"
Canyon Echo: "Sky Island Encounters," "Clear Sight"
Connecticut River Review: "Smoky Tango"
Cutthroat: "My Starling"
Eratica: "The Cavalier's Wife"
The New Verse News: "The Factory," "Without a Net," "The Man
    Next Door"
Pearl: "Biometrics in the Desert"
Poem: "Dismantling the Town"
The Poetry Conspiracy: "Writer's Block"
Presa: "Melancholia," "Trains at Rest," "The Wall Between"
The Rufous City Review: "The Unfinished Earth"
San Pedro River Review: "A Canyon View," "Afternoon Walk"
Sin Fronteras: "A Sense of Place"
Skidrow Penthouse: "One Look," "Freefall"
Slow Trains: "The Lost Teacher"
Spillway: "Undocumented Land"
Third Wednesday: "Traveling East Then South," "Silence," "Drought
    in the City"
Unstrung (The Blue Guitar): "Black Flight"
Voices on the Wind: "Mozart at the Hanging"

*Cover photo, "Madera Canyon on a Summer Evening," and author photo
by Roberta Chorlton; cover and interior book design by Diane Kistner
(dkistner@futurecycle.org); Gentium Book Basic with Cronos Pro titling*

About FutureCycle Press

FutureCycle Press is dedicated to publishing lasting English-language poetry books, chapbooks, and anthologies in both print-on-demand and Kindle ebook formats. Founded in 2007 by long-time independent editor/publishers and partners Diane Kistner and Robert S. King, the press incorporated as a nonprofit in 2012. A number of our editors are distinguished poets and writers in their own right, and we have been actively involved in the small press movement going back to the early seventies.

The FutureCycle Poetry Book Prize and honorarium is awarded annually for the best full-length volume of poetry we publish in a calendar year. Introduced in 2013, our Good Works projects are anthologies devoted to issues of universal significance, with all proceeds donated to a related worthy cause. Our Selected Poems series highlights contemporary poets with a substantial body of work to their credit; with this series we strive to resurrect work that has had limited distribution and is now out of print.

We are dedicated to giving all of the authors we publish the care their work deserves, making our catalog of titles the most diverse and distinguished it can be, and paying forward any earnings to fund more great books.

We've learned a few things about independent publishing over the years. We've also evolved a unique, resilient publishing model that allows us to focus mainly on vetting and preserving for posterity the most books of exceptional quality without becoming overwhelmed with bookkeeping and mailing, fundraising activities, or taxing editorial and production "bubbles." To find out more about what we are doing, come see us at www.futurecycle.org.